BUTTERFLIES

SEYMOUR SIMON

Collins
An Imprint of HarperCollins*Publishers*

Special thanks to the American Museum of Natural History,
for invaluable assistance.

PHOTO CREDITS: page 2: © Valerie Giles / Photo Researchers, Inc.; page 3: © Liz Nealon; page 4: © Mark Newman / Photo Researchers, Inc.; page 7, top: © Millard H. Sharp / Photo Researchers, Inc.; bottom: © John Mitchell / Photo Researchers, Inc.; page 8: © Stuart Wilson / Photo Researchers, Inc.; page 10, left: © E. R. Degginger / Photo Researchers, Inc.; middle: © Millard H. Sharp / Photo Researchers, Inc.; right: © Ray Coleman / Photo Researchers, Inc.; page 11: © Anthony Mercieca / Photo Researchers, Inc.; pages 12–13: © Kenneth M. Highfill / Photo Researchers, Inc.; page 14: © Valerie Giles / Photo Researchers, Inc.; page 15: © Perennou Nuridsany / Photo Researchers, Inc.; page 16: © Dr. Keith Wheeler / Photo Researchers, Inc.; page 17: © Cheryl Power / Photo Researchers, Inc.; page 19: © Adam Jones / Photo Researchers, Inc.; page 20: © Ray Coleman / Photo Researchers, Inc.; page 21, left to right: © Rod Planck / Photo Researchers, Inc.; © Gregory K. Scott / Photo Researchers, Inc.; © Richard and Ellen Thane / Photo Researchers, Inc.; © John Kaprielian / Photo Researchers, Inc.; page 23, top: © James H. Robinson / Photo Researchers, Inc.; bottom: © John Shaw / Photo Researchers, Inc.; page 24: © Jeff Lepore / Photo Researchers, Inc.; page 27: © James L. Amos / Photo Researchers, Inc.; page 28: © Kenneth H. Thomas / Photo Researchers, Inc.; page 31: © Adam Jones / Photo Researchers, Inc.
Collins is an imprint of HarperCollins Publishers.

Butterflies
Copyright © 2011 by Seymour Simon

Library of Congress Cataloging-in-Publication Data
Simon, Seymour.
Butterflies / Seymour Simon. — 1st ed.
p. cm.
ISBN 978-0-06-191493-5
1. Butterflies—Juvenile literature. I. Title.
QL544.2.S515 2011   2010032203
595.78'9—dc22   CIP
                                                                                        AC

11 12 13 14 15   SCP   10 9 8 7 6 5 4 3 2
❖
First Edition

As leaves change color in autumn, monarch butterflies begin an incredibly long journey to places they have never seen before. On tissue-paper-thin wings, the butterflies ride the wind as far as 3,000 miles to their winter homes.

The life span of a monarch is shorter than the time it takes to complete the migration every year. No one monarch makes the whole round-trip journey. Each autumn, the butterflies that travel to Mexico and Southern California are the great-grandchildren of butterflies that were born there. Yet somehow the monarchs know the routes that their ancestors took. Only some butterfly species, such as the North American monarchs, make such a long and difficult voyage, but many other butterflies and moths are remarkable creatures too.

Scientists have discovered and named more than one million creatures in the animal world. Insects make up more than three-quarters of all these known animals. About 18,000 to 20,000 kinds of butterflies and more than ten times as many kinds of moths have been identified. Butterflies and moths belong to a huge order of insects called Lepidoptera, meaning "scaly wings," because their wings are covered by thousands of tiny scales.

Butterflies and moths live in high mountains; in deserts and swamps; on cold, windblown Arctic tundra; and in warm tropical rainforests. They are important pollinators of flowers, and few butterflies or moths are pests. Butterflies also help the environment by providing food for animals such as bats, birds, lizards, and frogs.

Butterflies and moths are alike, but one way to tell the difference is to look at their antennae. A butterfly's antennae have a long shaft with a bulb, or knob, at the end. A moth's antennae are feathery, or saw-edged.

Butterflies are usually larger than moths and have bright colors on their wings. Moths most often are small and have dull-colored wings.

Butterflies and moths go through these four stages in their lives: egg, caterpillar, pupa, and adult. They look completely different during each stage, and each has a different purpose. Depending on the kind of butterfly or moth, the length of its life from the egg stage to the adult stage may be as short as a few weeks or as long as a few years.

The female usually attaches her eggs to a leaf or stem on or near a plant that serves as food for the future caterpillar. Some butterflies just drop their eggs in midflight over a grassy field. A female butterfly lays many eggs, sometimes more than a thousand. Only a few eggs will survive through an entire life cycle and become adults.

The egg hatches and becomes a caterpillar (or larva), the long, wormlike feeding stage of an insect. The caterpillar may have beautiful patterns of stripes or patches, and many have spinelike hairs covering their bodies. A butterfly caterpillar is constantly eating, tirelessly grinding and pulverizing food with its huge jaws. The caterpillar sheds its skin several times to keep pace with its rapidly growing body.

When a caterpillar is fully grown, it attaches itself to a stem or a branch by spinning a line of its own silk. In about twenty-four hours, the caterpillar sheds its skin for the last time and a pupa, or chrysalis, develops. A moth pupa is usually enclosed within a protective silk casing called a cocoon.

Although the pupa seems to be motionless, incredible things are going on inside the body. The pupa is the transformation stage of a butterfly's or moth's life cycle. The caterpillar tissues are being chemically broken down and reconstructed into those of an adult insect.

The pupa is usually brown or green and blends into the background against the plant leaves.

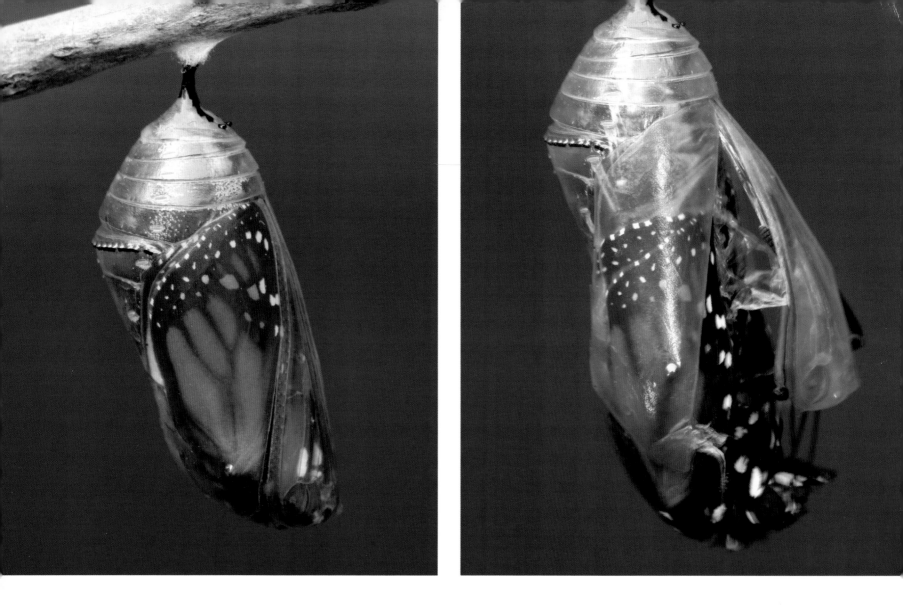

The pupa case cracks open and an adult butterfly emerges. It looks like a completely different creature than it was before. The butterfly gets rid of wastes from its body. The wings look crumpled at first. But when the butterfly pumps blood into them, the wings expand quickly and reach their full size in a few minutes.

The butterfly has to wait about an hour for its wings to harden

before it can fly. Usually a butterfly will fly straight to a plant and eat its first food since it was a caterpillar.

The adult (called an imago) is the colorful butterfly we usually see. An imago is the flying and reproductive stage of a butterfly or moth. An imago is either a male or a female. The male and female will court and mate and then the female will lay her eggs.

Butterflies and moths have three main body parts: the head, the thorax, and the abdomen. The head contains the eyes, the proboscis, and the antennae. Butterflies and moths have compound eyes made up of many

simple eyes that look in all directions—up, down, forward, backward, left, and right—all at the same time. They don't see things clearly the way we do, but they are able to see light and colors, even ultraviolet (which humans can't see). They can spot motion (as you probably know if you've ever tried to catch a butterfly in your hands).

Butterflies and moths can't bite or chew like caterpillars. They have a proboscis that is like a long tongue. They unroll their proboscis and use it like a straw to drink nectar from a flower or sap from a leaf or stem. The Morgan's sphinx moth has a proboscis 12 to 14 inches long.

Butterflies smell with their antennae and taste with their feet.

The thorax is the middle section of a butterfly or moth. Three pairs of jointed legs and two pairs of wings are attached to the thorax. Thousands of tiny scales cover every part of butterfly and moth bodies, but you can see the scales most easily on their wings. The brown powders on your fingers when you touch a butterfly are its scales. They are loosely attached and come off easily and without harm.

Colors and patterns on butterfly or moth wings help protect them from predators. The most common protection is camouflage, where the butterfly's wings blend in with tree bark, leaves, or stems.

Poisonous butterflies and moths often have bright colors that signal: "DANGER, KEEP AWAY." The "eye spot" on this owl butterfly makes it look like a much larger animal. Some butterflies have patterns that mimic, or look like, a poisonous species.

The rear part of a butterfly or moth, the abdomen, is softer than the rest of the body. It is divided into ten segments, some of which you can see easily. The abdomen contains a simple heart (more like a flexible tube that pumps blood), breathing pores (spiracles), the digestive and excretory systems, and either male or female reproductive organs.

Male and female butterflies often look alike, but some males are a bit smaller and more brightly colored. At mating time, male butterflies search for females that have the correct color and pattern on their wings. Then the male releases a powerful chemical called a pheromone, which attracts the female.

After mating, the female flies away in search of a plant on which to lay her eggs. She seems to recognize the right kind of plant by the color and shape of the leaves. Some butterflies lay one egg at a time, while others lay their eggs in clusters.

painted lady

Most regions of the United States are temperate, with warm summers and cold winters. When the weather warms up, you'll see butterflies on the wing. You may be able to spot about a hundred different kinds of butterflies not far from your home. Some common butterflies and their families in the United States are:

Brush-footed family: admiral, common wood nymph, painted lady, tortoiseshell, and viceroy.

Gossamer wing family: common and coral hairstreaks, spring azure.

Skipper family: common checkered and silver-spotted skippers.

Swallowtail family: giant, pipevine, and tiger swallowtails.

White and sulphur family: cabbage white and clouded, orange, and yellow sulphurs.

spring azure

silver-spotted skipper

pipevine

orange sulphur

Butterflies can be found in almost every place on Earth, but tropical rainforests are home to some of the most beautifully colored ones. Living conditions in these huge forests are ideal: It is warm and rainy all year round, and there are many flowering plants.

The blue morpho has large, brilliant blue wings about the size of your outspread hand. Sometimes a flutter of morpho butterflies looks like a blue cloud drifting among the treetops. Other gorgeous butterflies of South and Central American rainforests are the malachite (named after a beautiful blue-green mineral), the postman (they live up to nine months; the average life of a butterfly is less than one month), and the cattleheart.

Birdwing butterflies of tropical Southeast Asia are among the largest butterflies in the world. The Queen Alexandra's birdwing and the goliath birdwing are the size of a bird and fly like birds.

The dead leaf butterfly of Southeast Asia is a magnificent shining blue with orange markings. But when it folds up its wings, it looks exactly like a dead leaf.

There are 200,000 different kinds of moths. Most fly at night, but some fly during daylight hours. Among some cultures, certain moths are considered bad luck. People in parts of Mexico joke that if a black witch moth flies over your head, you will lose all your hair! A few kinds of moths are harmful, such as gypsy moths that eat crops and clothes moths that like to feast upon woolen clothing. Other kinds of moths, such as the silkworm, are useful.

North American giant silkworm moths have large lime-green wingspans of up to 4.5 inches and long hindwings with eye spots on them.

The North American polyphemus moth has a wingspan of 4 to 5 inches and belongs to the Saturniidae family. These moths have small or no tongues and can't feed as adults.

Unlike many other wild animals, butterflies and moths are easy to spot and observe in nature. Go outside in the warmer months of the year and find them in neighborhood gardens, meadows, vacant weedy lots, and the open edges of parks and woodlands.

With the aid of the photographs in this book or a butterfly field guide, try to identify the butterflies you see. Which group do they belong to? Are the butterflies you see solitary, or are there several of the same kind? Do the butterflies always alight on the same type of flower? You can keep a journal of your observations, photographs, and drawings. Be sure to record the date and time of day, the weather conditions (sunny or cloudy, windy or still, rainy or dry, and the temperature). You're working the way a scientist works when you keep a scientific journal.

If you have outdoor space around your school or home, you and your class or your family might want to make a "butterfly garden." The best garden for butterflies should be mostly sunny and not very windy. It should have flowering plants and bushes, and light-colored rocks, which can serve as butterfly "basking places."

Butterfly gardens should have different kinds of plants so that at least one kind is in bloom from early spring to late autumn. Some of the plants, trees, and shrubs native to the United States and Canada that you may want to plant include black-eyed Susan, milkweed, verbena, clover, phlox, coneflower, spice bush, hydrangea, and sumac.

Butterflies and moths have lived on Earth for many millions of years. The butterflies and moths that flew among the dinosaurs long ago look very much like those you see sipping nectar from flowers today.

In the United States, Canada, and Europe, many kinds of butterflies and moths are becoming rarer because the open fields and meadows where they live have disappeared. People view some butterfly food plants as weeds and destroy them. In rainforests, tropical butterflies are losing their homes.

Throughout human history butterflies and moths have been the subject of stories, myths, poetry, art, drama, and dance in many cultures. The Hopi Native Americans perform a ceremonial dance in homage to the butterfly. An Irish saying goes: "May the wings of the butterfly kiss the sun and find your shoulder to light on, to bring you luck, happiness and riches today, tomorrow, and beyond."

For many of us, butterflies are symbols of the wild loveliness and wonder of nature.

GLOSSARY

Abdomen—The third and last segment of a butterfly's or moth's body, containing the heart, the reproductive organs, and the digestive and excretory systems.

Antennae—A pair of long, thin, segmented sensory organs on a butterfly's or moth's head. Butterflies and moths use their antennae to smell and touch.

Chrysalis—The case or covering of a pupa.

Cocoon—The silk covering a moth larva forms around itself as it becomes a pupa.

Digestive system—The system that breaks down food into nutrients the body can use.

Excretory system—The system that gets rid of the body's waste products.

Imago—The adult stage of a butterfly or moth.

Larva—The early, growing stage of a butterfly or moth, when it is a caterpillar.

Lepidoptera—The order of insects that includes butterflies and moths. The name means "scaly wings."

Life cycle—The four stages that butterflies and moths go through in their lives: egg, larva, pupa, imago.

Migrate—To travel from one region to another as the seasons change.

Pheromone—A powerful chemical an animal releases to attract or influence the behavior of another animal of the same species.

Proboscis—A long feeding tube that butterflies and moths unroll and use to draw up nectar or water.

Pupa—The third stage of a butterfly or moth, when it is wrapped in its cocoon or chrysalis.

Spiracles—Tiny openings in a butterfly's or moth's body through which it breathes.

Thorax—The middle section of a butterfly's or moth's body where the legs and wings are attached.

INDEX

Bold type indicates illustrations.

Abdomen, 14, 18
Adult, 9, 12, 13
Antennae, 6, **7**, 14
Arctic, 6

Birdwing, 22
Black witch moth, 25
Blue morpho, 22
Breathing pores, 18
Brushfoot family, **20**, 21
Butterfly field guide, 26
Butterfly garden, **28**, 29

Camouflage, 17
Canada, 29, 30
Caterpillar, **8**, 9, 10
Cattleheart, 22
Chrysalis, 10, **10, 11, 12, 13**
Clothes moths, 25
Cocoon, 10, **10, 11**

Dead leaf butterfly, 22, **23**
Digestive system, 18

Egg, 9, 18
Excretory system, 18
Eyes, 14, **14, 15**

Feet, 14
Flying, 13
Food, 6, 9, 13, 30

Giant silkworm moths, 25
Goliath birdwing, 22
Gossamer wing family, 21, **21**
Gulf fritillary butterfly, **31**
Gypsy moths, 25

Hindwings, 25

Imago, 13, **13**
Insects, 6

Larva, **8**, 9
Lepidoptera, 6
Life cycle, 9
Luna moth, **7, 24**

Malachite, 22
Mating, 18, **19**

Mexico, 5, 25
Migration, 5
Monarch butterflies, **3, 4**, 5, **12, 13, 27**
Morgan's sphinx moth, 14

Nectar, 14, 30
North American monarchs, 5

Owl butterfly, **14, 16**, 17, **17**

Pheromone, 18
Poisonous, 17
Polyphemus moth, 25
Postman, 22
Predators, 17
Proboscis, 14, **15**
Pupa, 9, 10, **10, 11**, 12, **12**

Queen Alexandra's birdwing, 22

Reproductive organs, 18

Saturniidae family, 25
Scales, 6, 17
Scientific journal, 26
Silk, 10
Silkworm, 25
Skipper family, 21, **21**
South and Central American rainforests, 22
Southeast Asia, 22
Southern California, 5
Spiracles, 18
Stages, 9
Swallowtail family, 21, **21**

Temperate, 21
Thorax, 14, 17
Tropical rainforests, 6, 22

United States, 21, 29, 30

White and sulphur family, 21, **21**
Wings, 12, **16**, 17
Wingspan, 25

READ MORE ABOUT IT

www.seymoursimon.com
Seymour Simon's website

www.seymoursimon.com/index.php/for_educators/downloads
Educator guides for Seymour's books

www.butterfliesandmoths.org
Butterflies and Moths of North America

www.kidsbutterfly.org
The Children's Butterfly Site

GLOBAL WARMING
by Seymour Simon

TROPICAL RAINFORESTS
by Seymour Simon